CORNWALL
RAILWAY HERITAGE

John Stengelhofen

RAILWAYS were in many ways responsible for Cornwall becoming the holiday centre for millions. The 'Cornish Riviera' was invented and marketed by the publicity department of the Great Western Railway. The traffic generated has, since the last war, largely transferred to road, but the resorts that developed at the end of the last century were towns and villages served by the railway. Until the 1950s, additional Summer Saturday holiday specials were crowded with families, complete with bucket, spade and shrimp net, on their way from the big cities for a week on the sands at Newquay, St Ives, Bude or Perranporth.
Yet far earlier Cornwall had a small but significant place in the development of the steam train, while the building of the county's railways forms an unusual and fascinating story. The earlier part of this story is intimately connected with the industrial activity which resulted from the exploitation of Cornwall's immense mineral wealth, and the need to export tin and copper ores. Since the railways were originally tailored to these local needs, the county was the last in England to be connected to the national railway system; it was not until 1859 that it was possible to travel out of Cornwall by train, to Bristol, London or further afield.
The aim of this book is to briefly trace this story, while the gazetteer section describes the monuments of the railway age that remain to be seen in Cornwall.

EARLY DEVELOPMENTS IN STEAM

THE FIRST practical steam engine to move under its own power was a small model, only about 15 to 18" [38-45cm] long, which was made by William Murdoch in Redruth. Murdoch, a Scots engineer, chiefly remembered as the first person to use gas lighting in his house, was Boulton & Watt's resident engineer in Cornwall from 1779 to 1794. He was responsible for erecting their stationary steam engines for pumping and winding on Cornish tin and copper mines. In 1786 he produced a small model steam-propelled vehicle which ran, apparently causing widespread fear amongst the local population—including the Vicar of Redruth!

Cornwall's greatest engineer, Richard Trevithick, achieved major improvements in mine pumping engines, increasing their efficiency and so reducing the quantities of coal that had to be imported into the county—always a problem with Watt's engines in a county remote from sources of coal. He was responsible for the first use of high-pressure steam, which resulted in smaller and more powerful engines. By 1801 he had built his first steam carriage—and almost certainly the world's first mechanically propelled vehicle. Using high-pressure steam, the carriage first ran in Camborne on Christmas eve in that year, but 4 days later, while Trevithick and his partner were dining at an inn at Illogan the boiler boiled dry, overheated and the timber chassis caught fire, destroying the carriage.

Trevithick went on to build further carriages for use on the road, but in 1803 he became involved in a wager over the possibility of a steam locomotive hauling a load of 10 tons over a distance of 9¾ miles. The site of this trial, for which Trevithick built a locomotive, was the Pen-y-darren tramway in south Wales. The £500 wager was won, and so 10 years before George Stephenson's first locomotive, the world's first steam propelled railway train moved falteringly over the irregular track of this Welsh valley horse-tramway.

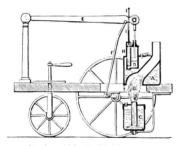

Section of Murdock's Model.

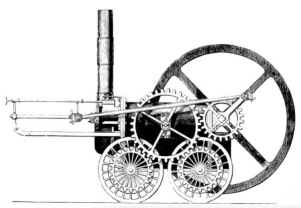

Trevithick's High Pressure Tram-Engine.

THE FIRST RAILWAYS

THE EARLIEST horse-drawn railways or tramways evolved in metal mines in central Europe and so it is not surprising that in Cornwall, known for its long history of metal mining, the first lines were built for the mines. The earliest recorded tramway in the county, underground in a tin-works near Pentewan, was in 1783, but it was the development of copper mining which resulted in most of the early railways above ground being built.

In Cornwall these first railways or tramways were, as elsewhere, horse-drawn and operated purely to move goods. In the far south-west the need for improved transport came chiefly from the mines; ores—particularly vast quantities of copper ore—had to be taken from inland mines, and coal for mine engines had to be brought back from the ports and harbours. These were the basic transport requirements of the county, and a number of small independent railway lines were built specifically to cater for these needs.

Cornwall at the beginning of the 19th century was far more remote than it is today and the quickest way to reach the capital was by sailing ship—in fine weather at least!

The population, barely 40% of todays, relied on agriculture, often on poor uplands and moors, on the mining of tin, copper and other minerals, on the quarrying of slate and granite and on the fast-developing china clay quarries. All these products, dug from the ground, had to be transported to distant markets. Transport from mine or quarry to the coast as well as the shipping from Cornwall's innumerable ports, harbours and sheltered coves were the elements of an infrastructure essential for this industrialisation. Steam pumping engines enabled mines to be successfully worked at greater depths so that production increased and furthered the demand for coal as a return cargo to supply mine pumping engines.

In 1800 all this transport had to rely on horses with side panniers—lengthy columns of mules would carry the ore— using steep and stoney tracks, few of which would merit the name 'road' today. Yet by the end of the century the county had exported huge quantities of bulky materials, much of it having been carried by rail for part of its journey; a million tons of tin, 9 million tons of copper ore and a similar quantity of china clay! It was these factors which dictated the routes of early railways in the county, rather than any need for passengers to travel to Bristol or London . . . . that would have to wait until 1859.

Before that date though, no fewer than 9 ports around the coast had been connected to a productive hinterland area by railways. Wadebridge, Newquay, Portreath, Hayle, Penzance, Devoran, Truro, Pentewan and Par all had railways by the 1850s, and, with the exception of Wadebridge, all of these lines were primarily built to serve a mining area.

Ore wagon underground in a Cornish tin mine, a scene little changed in 200 years.

POLDICE TRAMWAY

The earliest railway to be built above ground began at the small north coast harbour of Portreath, and served the mining area east of Redruth, particularly near St Day, mainly for the benefit of the United Mines and Poldice Mine, the latter giving the tramway its name. This little line, 4 miles long, was built to a gauge of about 4' 0".

Although the opening date is uncertain, the first rail was laid at Portreath in 1809 and it was in use as far as Scorrier House by 1812; it was probably completed by 1819. The tramway never had steam locomotives and never officially carried passengers; in fact it was a private railway built by the Williams family of Scorrier House for the use of mines in which they had an interest. It fell into disuse in the 1850s. Unlike any of the other railways in Cornwall, this was a plateway; that is to say, the rails were cast-iron with an **L**-section acting as a flange to guide the plain wheels of the wagons, unlike the modern railway where flanged wheels run on the top edge of the rail. These rails, made in short lengths, sat on granite sleeper blocks, as they did in several of the other early railways.

Miraculously, the small wagon designed for the use by the Directors of the line has survived, with two bench seats facing each other to carry just four people; apparently dating from the very early years of the line, this may well be the oldest surviving railway passenger carriage anywhere.

Redruth & Chasewater Railway locomotive *Miner* at Devoran.

REDRUTH AND CHASEWATER RAILWAY

Despite the success of the Poldice line it was more than ten years before another was built. John Taylor, the notable mining entrepreneur, had gained control of several major mines near St Day, including Consolidated and United Mines. Taylor introduced underground railways in many Cornish mines and soon realised the transport problems above ground. He therefore built a line, opened in 1826, running from Wheal Buller in the mining area to the south of Redruth with a branch into Redruth itself, connecting with the quays at Devoran, near Perran Foundry. Although it always kept its name, the Redruth and Chasewater Railway (with the old spelling for Chacewater), the proposed branch to Chacewater was never actually built.

The Directors' carriage of the Portreath Tramroad.

CORNWALL'S RAILWAY HERITAGE

Miner at the water tank near Carharrack.

Steam engines with names like *Miner* and *Smelter* were introduced to this 4' 0" gauge line in 1854, but passengers were never carried. In its peak years considerable quantities of ore were carried to the schooners waiting at Devoran or a mile further on at Point Quay, to which the line had been extended in 1827. During the last century the little hamlet of Devoran became one of the most important ports on the Cornish coast, with a two way trade—the export of copper and the import of coal.

With the decline in mining at the end of the 19th century, the railway's ultimate fate was sealed; from a peak traffic of 97,000 tons in 1865, it struggled on, traffic decreasing almost every year, until the first world war. The final train ran down the valley in September 1915.

Accident at Bissoe bridge.

PENTEWAN RAILWAY

The early decades of the last century saw the start of the china clay industry, which today provides the only regular bulk goods business in the county for British Rail. The problem of lack of ports in St Austell Bay was solved as harbours were built at Charlestown (1791) Pentewan (1826) and Par (1833).

All these were several miles from the clay pits, but Pentewan was the furthest, and so 4 years after it was opened, Sir Christopher Hawkins, the owner, built a railway leading up the valley to the town of St Austell. Despite numerous schemes to extend the line up into the clay district immediately to the north—the hilly country would have made it most difficult—it always stopped short. Heavy horse-drawn wagons had to bring the clay down to the railhead, a depot in the lower part of St Austell.

This narrow gauge line was operated by gravity for the first mile out of St Austell—the trains simply ran down the slope, usually in the charge of a boy who controlled the brake, and could bring the empty wagons back under horse power. The level part of the route down to Pentewan was then operated by horses in the early years. The gauge at that time was probably 4' 6", but in 1874 the line was rebuilt to 2' 6" gauge for the introduction of steam locomotives over the horse-worked section and then from 1907 the line into St Austell was steam worked throughout.

The earliest newspaper reference to the line working also recorded the first fatality on Cornwall's railways; in July 1829 a boy of 9 fell from the waggon he was 'driving', on the gravity-worked section, and was run over.

The Pentewan Railway's *Pioneer* brings a clay train down to the harbour in 1912. *late A.J.Fellows*

Passengers were never officially carried; but a single carriage was kept for the owner's use, and the sunday school outings from every chapel in the populous area around St Austell, to Pentewan beach, were a regular part of life in the clay district.

Pentewan was not an ideal port, being distant from the clay pits, but its major problem from the start was the silting which regularly blocked the entrance. Ships were trapped, having to wait for the next spring tide. Improvements to processing within the clay industry gave other ports advantages, and the rise of Fowey, with its GWR jetties, combined with Pentewan's worsening silt problems reduced trade to the port. The railway was closed in 1918, and a few years later the last commercial ship left.

Early this century the company who were then operating the harbour began manufacturing concrete building blocks, using the wind-blown dune sand; this operation continued until the 1960s, and the remaining track still to be seen at Pentewan dates from this period, when diesel locomotives were used.

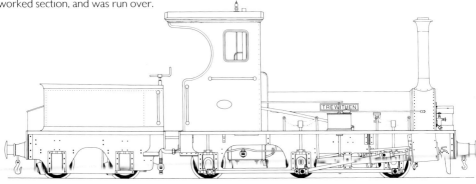

TREWITHEN (tender drawn from photographs)

A Sunday School treat to Pentewan in the early years of this century.

BODMIN & WADEBRIDGE RAILWAY

Of the early lines the Bodmin and Wadebridge was the first to be built to the so-called standard gauge of 4' 8½"; it was the first to use steam locomotives from its inception; it was the first built for imports rather than exports—and it was the first to carry passengers.

The purpose of the line was to carry seasand inland to 'sweeten' the fields. Much of the west country suffers from over-acid soil and one of the earliest methods of correcting this was by spreading sand. That from the north coast, high in calcium—crushed shells—was of particular note. The line ran from Wadebridge, where the company built a new quay, along the River Camel to Wenford, a distance of 12 miles, with branches to Bodmin and Ruthern Bridge and was opened in 1834.

Passengers were carried from the beginning, and a year before Thomas Cook ran his first excursion, special trains were being run to view public hangings at Bodmin Jail, conveniently situated alongside the line just short of the station.

The first rather crude locomotive, named *Camel*, arrived by sea across the Bristol Channel, from Neath Abbey Ironworks, and despite teething problems soon proved itself a success. Although stationary steam engines were com-

```
Bodmin & Wadebridge
        Railway.
  290
EXCURSION TICKET.
   NOT TRANSFERABLE.

JULY 18th, (1s.) 1876.
```

oped, with granite from quarries on the edge of Bodmin Moor and iron ore from mines around Bodmin. By the 1860s china clay pits were being developed on the moor, and so Wadebridge became another clay port. This was later to become the main business on the Wenford line, where lengthy clay 'dries' were built, continuing in use until closure of the line in 1983.

The years of independence were limited however, for in 1846 the line was acquired by the London & South Western Railway, although as we shall see, that company did not physically connect with its new line for 49 years!

mon in the county's mines, it must be remembered that this was advanced technology for the time as the nearest other steam locomotives then operating were in Leicestershire and Kent! A second locomotive followed shortly afterwards, being given the name *Elephant*, ... a seemingly logical companion for *Camel*, as far as the makers were concerned, unaware that the first was named after the river which also gives its name to Camelford!

Despite these unusual features, the Bodmin & Wadebridge settled down as a remote rural railway, carrying sand inland to be sold from its depots or 'wharves', while other traffic devel-

Bodmin & Wadebridge milestone.

A Bodmin & Wadebridge Railway Directors' special at Bodmin in the 1880s. *Cornish Studies Library*

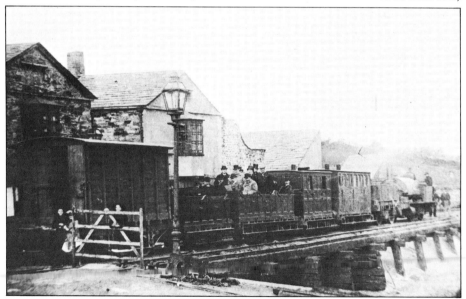

THE HAYLE RAILWAY

Of more lasting significance, the Hayle Railway was also the first passenger carrying line in west Cornwall. It too was primarily aimed at serving the mines around Camborne and Redruth and the ports of Hayle and Portreath. Forming the basis of the West Cornwall Railway, apart from certain diversions, this line eventually became part of the GWR main line from Penzance to Paddington and continues in use today.

The Hayle Railway, from its opening in 1837, was locomotive worked between Hayle and Portreath—although the descent to that Harbour was by a rope worked incline powered by a stationary steam engine; there was a similar incline at Angarrack just east of Hayle. The line below these inclines was worked by horses, but the main section was locomotive-worked, as were the branches to Roskear and Crofty, and into the old station at Redruth, opened in 1843, when passenger services began on the line. The main route however, branched south of the present day line, reaching numerous mines around Tresavean by another incline, although locomotives worked up this incline as they did on the shorter Penponds incline west of Camborne.

A special outing to Caradon Hill about 1903.

THE LISKEARD RAILWAYS

In the east of the county, huge deposits of copper ore were discovered in 1836, and to help exploit these and nearby granite quarries—notably the Cheesewring Quarry—the Liskeard and Caradon Railway was built.

It ran from the Cheesewring down to a point roughly under the Moorswater viaduct on the Cornwall Railway main line, where it connected with the Liskeard and Looe Canal which had been opened in 1827-8. South of Minions village

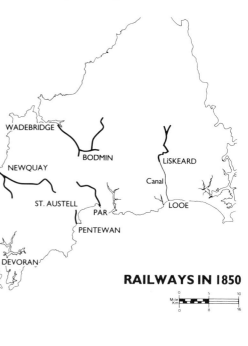

RAILWAYS IN 1850

on the Cheesewring line was the rope worked Gonamena incline, but otherwise the line was simply worked by gravity. Loaded waggons were run down to Moorswater, in charge of a 'brakesman' and the empty waggons were then hauled back by horses the next morning. This system worked from the opening of the line in 1844 until 1872, when the Tokenbury line was extended in a loop around Caradon Hill to join the Cheesewring branch; the incline was then abandoned and steam locomotives introduced.

The Liskeard & Looe Union Canal Co. operated a railway longer than it did a canal, for in 1860 their railway opened, replacing the canal, from its junction with the Liskeard and Caradon, down to the quays at East Looe; they did not change their name (to Liskeard and Looe *Railway*) until 1895! Initially the line was worked by the Caradon company, but as their finances deteriorated, the roles were reversed. The Liskeard & Looe, over whose line the LCR had introduced a passenger service in 1879, leased the Caradon line from 1901 until working was taken over by the GWR in 1909. In 1917 the Caradon lines were abandoned and in 1923 the Looe line was vested totally in the GWR.

Although there was almost 150' [45m] difference in levels between Moorswater and the main line above, a connection would have been an obvious advantage particularly for the convenience of passengers, but a number of schemes were put forward before the present circuitous loop was built in 1901, This ends at a new platform adjoining, but virtually at right angles to, the existing Liskeard station. This is still the departure point for the diesel units on the Looe branch.

A Looe train at Moorswater station, Liskeard & Caradon Railway, in the early 1880s. The locomotive is *Caradon*, built in 1862.

Treffry Viaduct.

TREFFRY'S TRAMWAYS

Joseph Thomas Treffry was an innovative entrepreneur, with interests in mining, quarrying and china clay as well as being a substantial landowner. He built Par harbour, and then, to improve transport to his various enterprises he built two tramways. The first of these lead from an area of clay pits around Bugle through Luxulyan to Ponts Mill, at the bottom of the narrow Luxulyan Valley, where clay and stone was transshipped to a short length of canal which connected with Par Harbour.

The other route connected clay pits near St Dennis with a small fishing village which had recently had its harbour extended and been bought by Treffry in 1837. The village was named after a 'new' quay built hundreds of years before: Newquay. In addition a branch to East Wheal Rose served that prosperous lead and silver mine near Newlyn East.

There is some uncertainty when these horse-drawn lines were completed, but by 1850 both were busy carrying china clay, minerals and stone. The delays in transshipment at Ponts Mill soon resulted in the tramway being extended down the mile or so to Par harbour.

The engineering problems in reaching the high ground from Par were considerable, but the solution was ingenious and has left what is probably the single most interesting and spectacular monument of Cornwall's 19th century industrial development, and a fitting memorial to its builder. With horse-drawn trains, gradients are critical, and so the rise was concentrated in one major incline, just above Ponts Mill, to be worked by water power—which was always Treffry's preference, if a source of water was available. This brought the line up 325' [99m], but on the east side of the valley, which then had to be crossed by a viaduct. A substantial water supply existed at a high level on the west side of the valley and this was needed to work the incline water-wheel. A combined viaduct/aqueduct was therefore built, 100' [30m] high, crossing the valley; it is almost certainly the largest structure in the country for this dual purpose. The tail-water from the incline wheel then joined the main leat to Fowey Consols, Treffry's copper mine, which again made full use of water wheels for pumping and winding ore.

The first section of tramway was built from the Colcerrow stone quarry to the site of the viaduct when construction began, massive cut granite blocks being used. Work was completed in 1842, and although the tramway has long since been closed, the standard of design and workmanship is illustrated by the use to this day of the water channel under what was the trackbed.

After Treffry's death in 1850, the tramway continued for a further 22 uneventful years, before ambitious proposals were put forward for new steam railways in mid-Cornwall which would incorporate Treffry's tramways.

ARRIVAL OF A MAIN LINE

THE SPARSE population and limited potential traffic levels, together with the hilly nature of the country, meant that building mainline railways to the west country was costly with no guarantee of profits, or even an adequate return on investments for the railway companies.

Added to this there was competition between two major companies, which sometimes resulted in a division of what traffic there was — although this affected Devon more particularly. Both the Great Western Railway from Paddington and the London & South Western Railway from Waterloo attempted to provide the far southwest with a main line service; although it was the GWR who 'won' the battle in most of Cornwall, it was the L&SWR who gained the first foothold in the county.

During the 1840s numerous proposals were made for mainline railways into the county, two routes being favoured; either a central along the spine of the county from Launceston to Bodmin and Truro, or a route nearer to the south coast from Plymouth through Liskeard and St Austell to Truro. The 1845 proposal for a 'Central Cornwall Railway' was to incorporate branches of the Bodmin & Wadebridge Railway in a line from Exeter and Launceston to Truro. Although backed by the L&SWR, the scheme failed, but the Bodmin & Wadebridge was bought out in 1846. The takeover was not in fact made legal with the required parliamentary approval for 40 years, and there was no physical link with the L&SWR system until 1895.

The GWR, with Isambard Kingdom Brunel as engineer, was also extending westward, through its 'associated companies' — effectively subsidiaries, although developed out of locally-based companies. These lines had his 7' 0" gauge, the magnificent and far-sighted 'broad-gauge'. The Bristol and Exeter Railway reached Exeter in 1844 and the South Devon was open through to Plymouth in 1849. The standard gauge (4' 8½") L&SWR line from Waterloo via Salisbury reached Exeter in 1860 and arrived at Plymouth in 1876, initially over GWR track, but then with its own line from Lydford after 1890.

Just as the L&SWR — and the Liberals in the county — backed the Central Cornwall route, so the GWR — and the Tories — backed broad gauge schemes taking the southern route. Although avoiding crossing the edge of Bodmin Moor, this entailed lengthy viaducts to cross the river valleys of the south coast, but would better serve the populations of Liskeard, St Austell and Truro and give them access to Plymouth.

In 1846 the Cornwall Railway obtained its Act of Parliament, with a scheme for the 'southern' route laid out by Brunel, following failure in the previous year. Although backed by the GWR, this company now had many local Cornish directors, and the chairman of the company was J.T.Treffry. The first sod was cut at Truro in August 1847, after which little was to be done for some years.

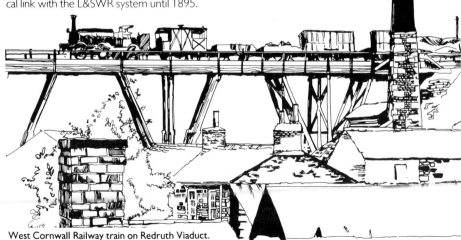

West Cornwall Railway train on Redruth Viaduct.

WEST CORNWALL RAILWAY

AT THE SAME time proposals were made to extend the little Hayle Railway—in both directions—to form the West Cornwall Railway, connecting Truro and Penzance. This involved modernising it and converting to broad gauge, while diverting the line to avoid the Angarrack and Penponds inclines with their rope hauled trains and stationary steam engines. Although this line, through Redruth, Camborne and Hayle, had better potential, covering the county's main areas of population and industry, the promoters still had difficulty raising the finance. They opted to keep the standard gauge of the Hayle Railway as an economy, despite being decidedly in the broad gauge camp, and financially supported by the GWR and its associated companies.

The WCR took over the Hayle line in 1846 but it was not until 1852 that they were able to close it briefly for the final conversion work; the new line was open from Penzance to Redruth in March of that year and through to Truro in August. Truro now had a railway, no small factor in the gradual transfer of county town status from Bodmin, which (apart from the little Bodmin & Wadebridge line), was only usefully served, after 1887, by a branch from the main line some 4 miles away.

Mineral traffic, particularly from mines around Camborne and Redruth to Hayle, was vitally important, as it had been with the Hayle Railway, although this traffic was to begin a decline after the 1860s. The importance of this traffic is indicated by their having 300 wagons, while the longer route of the Cornwall Railway only 100.

Excursions began as early as 1852, with the Chapel and Temperance outings which were such a feature of life in 19th century Cornwall:

> Happy Camborne, Happy Camborne,
> Where the railway is so near;
> And the engine shows how water
> Can accomplish more than beer.

The WCR speeded up the journey to London for it was now possible to travel from Penzance or Truro to Hayle, take the paddle steamer packet service to Bristol and continue by rail to the metropolis. It was to be seven years before the through link was to be completed—between Truro and Plymouth.

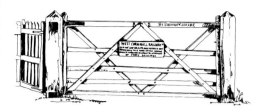

THE CORNWALL RAILWAY

THE CONNECTING route, the broad gauge line through Cornwall, was to involve one major and many minor engineering problems.

Over 4 miles [8%] of the original route was to be on some form of viaduct or bridge and this problem, common to other lines in Devon and south Wales, caused Brunel to design a basic viaduct, using a complex construction of timber members to span between the stone piers; 34 of these were used between Truro and Plymouth. Known as 'fan viaducts' from the form of the timber work above the masonry piers, they were comparatively cheap to build, and, in theory, it was easy to maintain or even replace individual timbers. The standard design used so extensively in Cornwall proved very costly to maintain; the need to double the main line, resulted in their gradual replacement from 1871 onwards. To avoid interruption of traffic, the new all-stone and brick viaducts had to be built alongside the old, the actual track being moved over finally during a weekend. Afterwards the timberwork was removed but in most cases the piers of Brunel's structures remain a few yards from the new.

With 6 miles of viaduct to be renewed in this way on the Cornwall and West Cornwall lines, the job was spread over many years and the last of the fan viaducts, College Wood, near Penryn, on the Falmouth branch was not replaced until 1934.

The major engineering work upon which the link depended was spanning the river Tamar, the boundary between Devon and Cornwall. With 1100' [335m] of water and the necessity for 100' [30m] clear height at high water, to give clearance for naval vessels on the river, the problem was considerable; the resulting, unique, structure was an economic solution which remains a major memorial to Brunel.

Replacing Collegewood Viaduct, on the Falmouth branch with a new masonry structure, 1933-34.
Royal Institution of Cornwall

After the years of delay, and the revived threat of a central line, the GWR, B&E and SDR came to the rescue of the Cornwall Railway and work progressed during the later 1850s. Finally the official opening of the bridge by Prince Albert came on the 2nd of May, 1859. Services started two days later, between Truro and the South Devon Railway's terminus at Plymouth, Millbay, 13 years after parliamentary consent had been given for the line. The Millbay terminus of the Cornwall Railway was close to the present Ferry Terminal, which is situated in Brunel's Millbay dock, originally built for the GWR.

Financial problems, and in particularly the bankruptcy of the contractor, resulted in even further delays on the Truro to Falmouth section, which was opened three years later. Falmouth's importance, in transport terms, was already in decline, for since the Cornwall Railway had first been mooted the Royal Mail Packet Services had been transferred to Southampton after more than 150 years. The result of all this was that Falmouth did not become, as intended, a continuation of the main line, but has always operated as a local branch.

THE BREAK OF GAUGE

IN 1859 Truro therefore had two railways, a short branch of the West Cornwall line from Penzance having been built to connect with the new (present day) Truro Station, which soon superseded the old Newham Station for passenger services. Truro also had a 'break of gauge'. No through passenger trains could operate, and goods had to be transshipped from the standard gauge West Cornwall to the broad gauge Cornwall—and vice versa!

It was a situation experienced elsewhere at the borders of GWR territory, where there was no alternative until the conversion of the broad and standardisation of gauges. Here though, all that was needed was the addition of a third rail, so that both 4' 8½" and 7' 0" trains could run over the 25 miles of otherwise isolated track.

Even this was to prove beyond the resources of the poor WCR, though it was a requirement in their Act of Parliament. When the CR gave notice that they wanted the third rail laid, it was the end of the independent company; in 1866 it was taken over by the broad gauge companies,

Broad gauge train at Redruth.

the third rail laid and through services started on the 1st of March 1867. Points were required to ensure that narrow gauge trains were brought to the face of the platforms, and — unique amongst mixed gauge lines — the WCR was to run mixed goods trains with some broad and some narrow gauge wagons, which must indeed have been a strange sight.

Evidence presented to the Parliamentary Commission set up in 1845 to look at the merits of the two gauges showed the superior performance of Brunel's line and Daniel Gooch's locomotives. But the practical difficulties of numerous breaks of gauge at a time when the country's trade was booming as never before, made it an economic necessity to have one 'standard' gauge throughout the kingdom. The 4' 8½" was already widespread in the midlands, north and east and, as a result, parliament limited broad gauge expansion to the southwest and south wales. Conversion to standard gauge was begun in 1866. In the west, however, the services of the GWR and associated companies were effectively blighted by the doomed system for a further 47 years until the final conversion of the stronghold of Brunel's magnificent railway — west of Exeter — in 1892.

It may be truer to say potentially magnificent; during this period the opportunities were lost and it was never shown what could be done with a railway built to a larger scale than any other in the world. There was no incentive to fully develop locomotives, for instance, and the last broad gauge expresses were hauled by rebuilt versions of Gooch's designs of the 1840s. With 8' diameter single driving wheels and a chimney with copper top, which towered 15' over the rails, these locomotives were capable of over 70 mph. They had developed from the *Great Western*, which ran from Paddington to Exeter via Bristol, in 1846, in 208 minutes for the 194 miles, an average of 56 mph. In the 1840s these speeds were far in advance of anything achieved on other railways. They had undoubtedly been far in advance of their time when built, but locomotive engineering elsewhere was developing fast in these early years, and few other designs survived for nearly 50 years.

For use on the hilly curved lines in the west, which had been laid out for working by the atmospheric system which was less affected by gradients, Gooch designed his 4-4-0 saddle tanks, built originally for the South Devon Railway. Although less spectacular, they were powerful-looking engines, well suited to the lines and, again, destined to haul expresses in the decades up to 1892. The Cornwall Railway never possessed any locomotives of its own, as these were supplied initially by the contractor who supplied the South Devon, and then after 1866 by the South Devon itself. In common with the WCR, the Cornwall Railway suffered from a low level of business and was always short of finances. This resulted in poor track

The last through broad gauge train to Penzance about to leave Paddington, 20th May 1892.

maintenance and trains which were known to roll violently. In addition there was the bad publicity of an accident on the second day of working, when a locomotive came off the track approaching a viaduct near St Germans and landed with its funnel stuck in the river mud below.

Train services were unnecessarily slow, taking 12 hours from Penzance to Paddington when through trains first began. It was worse for third class passengers, who were excluded from express trains and given little protection from the weather, even for a journey from Paddington to Penzance, which would last from 13 to 15¼ hours (an average of 21 mph compared with 62.8 today); after 1869 third class pasasengers were allowed on one 12 hour train a day. Economic working was more important than speed and South Devon engine-drivers, with an incentive bonus to reduce their coal consumption, would coast down hill!

Telegraph was installed at the beginning to control the single line sections between stations, but with rudimentary signalling trains left stations on a verbal instruction. This resulted in one accident in 1873; Richard being a favoured christian name in the county, the 'Right away, Dick' signal, resulted in *two* trains leaving Menheniot Station at the same time. The up train was then involved in a head-on collision on the single line section, killing one driver and damaging *Lance* beyond repair. A major contribution to the safety record—there was not a single passenger fatality—must have been the slow train speeds in these early years. Even in the 1870s, the fastest train from Truro to Plymouth averaged 15.8 mph while, still limited by the difficult route and frequent stops, trains today manage three times this speed.

The considerable impact of the arrival of the main line is difficult to appreciate nowadays, but it affected all aspects of life in the county. Towns on the line developed, while those that were by-passed went into decline. Early crops, particularly flowers, which the county's mild climate encouraged, could now be distributed to London and other major centres of population. Fishing found new markets for fresh fish, to replace the mediterranean markets for salted pilchards, and those ports close to railways, notably Newlyn, prospered. Standard time had to be introduced for running railways and this replaced local time which varied from town to town. This was not always welcomed, and a third red minute hand on some town clocks indicated the new London or railway time, about 15 minutes behind local time.

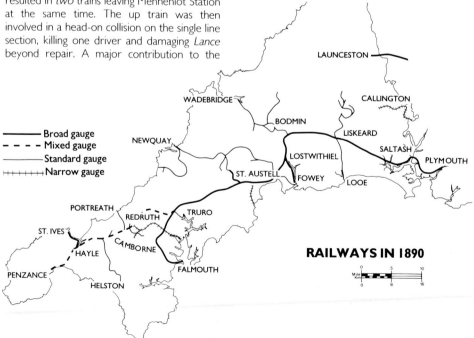

RAILWAYS IN 1890

THE GREAT WESTERN RAILWAY

IN REALITY, despite Cornish directors on the board and even local Chairmen, both sections of the Cornish main line had for long been operated by the Great Western Railway, in the form of some joint committee with its associated broad gauge companies. In 1866 the West Cornwall was absorbed by the associated companies and a rent paid which was enough to pay a dividend to the shareholders, until the company was dissolved in 1878. The Cornwall Railway was finally taken over by the GWR in 1889, after previous attempts had been stopped by those who were speculating in the company's shares.

These changes made little difference until the conversion of the gauge from Exeter to Penzance over a weekend in May 1892, when 4200 workmen from all over the GWR system were assembled for this major undertaking. With the sad end, the last broad gauge trains cleared the county of the old wagons and carriages:

> And as each station-master saw the red
> lamps, burning bright,
> Recede into the darkness, and silence of
> the night,
> He wrung his hands in agony, and smote
> his breast,
> To see the last of Broad Gauge trains pass
> to its final rest.

Standard gauge trains were taken down over the L&SWR lines for the first up trains on the Monday morning. There was widespread nostalgia in the two counties for Brunel's great railway experiment, but the improvements which soon followed must have been ample compensation.

The Cornishman became the first corridor lavatory train in the west, and after 1893 timetables were gradually improved. By 1904 the *Cornish Riviera Express* was introduced, and for 20 years held the world record for the longest non-stop run, from Paddington to Penzance; it also reached Penzance in 7 hours although it became known as the 'Limited' because of the restriction to six coaches. Locomotives were now developed, the single wheelers, some specially designed to be converted from broad to standard gauge, giving way to 4-4-0s and then to 4-6-0s able to take faster yet heavier expresses on the long hard haul to the west as passenger numbers increased, especially on summer Saturdays. Restaurant cars were made available to 2nd and 3rd class passengers in 1903 and 2nd was abolished in 1910.

After 1906, the 'cut-off' line via Castle Cary reduced the distance from London to the west by some 20 miles, avoiding the long route through Swindon and Bristol—or the 'Great Way Round' as it was known to some! Apart from the war years, from then until nationalisation and the end of steam, most of the system altered little. Timetables remained similar over the years, apart from additional trains, particularly to Newquay, on summer Saturdays. The classic GWR locomotives, the Stars, Cities, Counties, and then the Castles of 1923 and (east of Plymouth) the Kings of 1927, perpetuated in jig-saw puzzles, post-cards and books, were to continue to carry main line trains to Cornwall up to the introduction of diesel—and for many months after, when trains were stranded by their unreliable successors!

The first 'Cornish Riviera Express' leaving Penzance, 1904. *Royal Institution of Cornwall*

OTHER STEAM RAILWAYS

CORNWALL MINERALS RAILWAY

Largely on the strength of opening up large scale iron mines there developed a need for improved transport in the area, with a through connection between the mines and both ports of Par and Newquay. The Cornwall Minerals Railway obtained its Act of Parliament in 1873 with powers to take over Treffry's tramways. There were to be various alterations to the route, for working by steam locomotives, and some level crossings were replaced by bridges; a section of line was added, to join the two parts of the tramway while there was to be an extension to Fowey, an extension of the East Wheal Rose branch to Treamble Mill and two branches into the clay district (Carbis and Retew). The alterations included a deviation to avoid a tunnel near St Columb Road, and new track leading up the Luxulyan valley (at about the steepest possible gradient of 1 in 37) thus avoiding the Carmears Incline and the Treffry Viaduct.

On 1 June 1874—just 11 months after the Act of Parliament—the lines were open. A new depot and engineering works was built at St Blazey, for this was a small railway system of over 40 miles which, being standard gauge, was isolated by the GWR's broad gauge.

Passenger trains started to operate between Fowey and Newquay in 1874, but the line's traffic never reached anticipated levels, and an agreement was made for the GWR to work the line from 1877. The system was amalgamated with the GWR in 1896, and, with the efforts of the Paddington publicity machine, was soon to become the premier holiday route.

EAST CORNWALL MINERAL RAILWAY

Callington, Calstock and the Tamar valley had long felt the need for a railway connection with the outside world and after a number of proposals a line was opened from Kelly Bray, near Callington, to Calstock in 1872. This 3' 6" gauge line passed a number of mines, brickworks and quarries on the high ground around Kit Hill and Gunnislake before descending by a rope-worked incline to the quays at Calstock which at the time was still a busy port.

But there was still the need for a line which lead out of the Tamar valley, rather than relying on the river steamers connecting with Plymouth. This was to come after the Plymouth, Devonport and South Western Junction Railway took over the line in 1891 and planned a short connection with their line at Bere Alston on the Devon side of the river. A fine new viaduct was built at Calstock, the line then looping to connect with the ECMR just above the top of the incline. Form here to Kelly Bray—renamed Callington—it took the old route which was rebuilt to standard gauge. Only the incline up the side of Kit Hill, leading to the granite quarry was to remain at the old 3' 6" gauge, and now forms a steep footpath approach to Kit Hill.

This new line, with a passenger service, was opened in 1908 giving connections to Plymouth and, by the L&SWR expresses, from Bere Alston to Waterloo. After 1923 the branch was operated by the Southern Railway. Proposals to close the line were strongly opposed because of the geographical isolation of the Tamar valley and difficulties of alternative road transport. The compromise solution saw the closure of the section between Callington and Gunnislake in 1966, but a passenger service from there, through Calstock to Plymouth.

Latchley ECMR depot

LATER GWR BRANCHES

MENTION MUST be made of other branches which were added to the GWR system in later years.

TO ST IVES

The short branch to St Ives is notable as being the last new broad gauge line to be built, opening in 1877, only 15 years before the conversion to standard gauge.

This scenic route along the edge of St Ives Bay from the junction at St Erth is the busiest branch line remaining. Apart from extra summer traffic connected with the park-and-ride service, even the winter schedules have 19 trains daily each way.

THE HELSTON RAILWAY

A local company, the Helston Railway was set up in 1880 to build a branch to that town from a junction with the main GWR line at Gwinear Road. The GWR worked the line from its opening in 1887 and took over the company completely in 1898. This line was one of the many casualties of the severe cuts under the Beeching plan, but a goods service continued one year longer, until 1963, with early vegetables providing considerable traffic. The spring congestion on the roads around Nancegollan station, caused by tractors and trailers loaded with brocolli, was then replaced by congestion on the roads all the way to Covent Garden.

Holiday crowds pack the platform in this early view of St. Ives.   *Cornish Studies Library*

Praze station.   *Cornish Studies Library*

A steam rail-motor at St. Agnes, about 1920. *Cornish Studies Library*

TO BODMIN

Also in 1887 an isolated standard gauge branch was built from the main line (broad gauge for another five years) at Bodmin Road station into the town of Bodmin, which had long suffered from its lack of a main railway connection. The new Bodmin General station was on the south side of the town, and a year later a loop line joined this to Boscarne Junction on the Bodmin & Wadebridge which entered the town from the north.

Along with the main North Cornwall lines, the passenger service was withdrawn in 1967, but goods traffic continued until 1983.

CHACEWATER & NEWQUAY

The last addition to the system was an alternative route to Newquay, from near Chacewater on the main line, through the heart of the holiday areas. Officially the Truro & Newquay Railway, the service normally operated between those stations, leaving Truro for Chacewater and on to a new junction at Blackwater. It then called at St Agnes, Perranporth and a number of halts before connecting with the Treamble mineral line at Shepherds, by which route it entered Newquay. The 7¾ miles to Perranporth was opened in 1903, and the 4½ mile link to Shepherds followed two years later. The Chacewater to Newquay line, although fairly well used, was closed completely in 1963.

Goonhavern Halt.

THE CHINA CLAY LINES

Just as Cornwall's metal mines spawned some interesting railways so did the china clay industry, which was only developing on a large scale in the latter part of the last century. Some of these lines were incorporated in later railways, such as the Cornwall Mineral Railway (now the Newquay branch), but others were lines purely in the clay district itself. These are covered in the gazetteer section of this book.

The transport of china clay mostly depends on shipping, for a high percentage has always been exported. As ships increased in size, the deep-water facilities at Fowey became better suited to this traffic, and so it shares the trade with Par. Both ports depended on the railway connections for their development, and continue to be served, while the English China Clays company remains the only regular provider of goods traffic on any scale for Cornwall's railways. With purpose-built wagons, huge quantities of clay are transported within Cornwall and further afield, as well, by regular services to the Potteries.

G.W.R.

BUGLE

A typical Great Western branch line train, at Bugle about 1900.
Cornish Studies Library

THE OTHER TRUNK ROUTE

THE AIM of the London and South Western Railway, in its early support of the Central Cornwall Railway and its purchase of the Bodmin and Wadebridge Railway, was to reach the depths of the south-west by a standard gauge trunk route from Waterloo in London.

In 1846 when the Central Cornwall Bill was rejected, and the B&W purchased, the L&SWR had only built its own main line from London as far as Basingstoke; it did not even reach Exeter until the year after the completion of the Cornwall Railway, in 1860. The progress through Devon, by a route skirting the northern edge of Dartmoor at levels up to 950', was slow; after Okehampton, Lydford was reached in 1874 and thence by way of GWR track, through trains to Plymouth began two years later. With their associated company, the Plymouth Devonport & South Western Junction Railway, they had a separate route into Plymouth from 1890. This line was operated by the L&SWR, although the PD&SWJR themselves only operated the Callington branch line, which was an extension of the earlier narrow gauge East Cornwall Mineral Railway.

Entry into north Cornwall, which was to become—even if briefly—L&SWR territory, began towards the end of the century. Despite the earlier proposals for 'central' railways, and even an Act of Parliament in 1864 for a Launceston, Bodmin and Wadebridge Junction Railway, it was under an Act of 1882 that the North Cornwall Railway was begun, as a L&SWR subsidiary.

From Halwill Junction it just reached over the Tamar to the border town of Launceston in 1886. By stages, the building of the line continued across the flat north Cornwall countryside, reaching the vast Delabole slate quarry which was to be a major user of the line in the years to come; its production of 10,000 tons a year was to be sent away by L&SWR wagons. Camelford was reached in 1893 and Wadebridge in 1895, at last making contact with the Bodmin & Wadebridge Railway. The further extension to the small harbour village of Padstow followed in 1899. During these last years of the century, plans for any westward extensions to Truro were forgotten.

Further up the coast, Bude had a branch of its own, from Halwill Junction, opened in 1898. But the harbour at this remote village of 1000 people was by then of little importance and the canal was disused. With the railway it would develop as a holiday resort, but would never be in the same league as Newquay.

When the North Cornwall arrived, the small towns of the area had been backwaters too long; the train service was slow and lengthy and the places it served have never caught up with towns on the southern route—where the railway had already been a part of life for some 40 years. The north of Cornwall, having waited up to 50 years for a railway, only saw it last for 70

Crowds rush to greet the first train to arrive at Padstow, 1899.   *Royal Institution of Cornwall*

years, since all the Southern Railway lines west of Okehampton were withdrawn as part of the shortsighted actions of British Railways in 1967.

The *Atlantic Coast Express* never truly competed with the *Cornish Riviera Express*, stopping for through carriages to be taken off for Bude, Ilfracombe, Torrington, Plymouth and Padstow. From Exeter none of these routes seemed to be more than a branch, and, excepting Plymouth, served small towns generating little enough traffic to justify an express from London. After nationalisation, in 1961 for instance, the 11.00am from Waterloo actually bettered by 2 minutes the fastest train from Paddington as far as Exeter; this was further improved by 30 minutes in the final years of steam. Exeter to Plymouth then took 25 minutes longer than by the GWR route. Carriages which were destined for Padstow took 381 minutes for the 259 miles, while by the old GWR route, a similar distance (Paddington to Par) was reached in 302 minutes although this is now reached in 225 minutes!

The L&SWR became part of the Southern Railway, although few changes were to be made between the wars. More and more the line relied on holiday traffic, but never to the same extent as the GWR; the same trains trundled slowly through the sparsely populated area, calling at now-forgotten little stations—St Kew Highway, Port Isaac Road, Otterham, Tresmeer and Egloskerry.

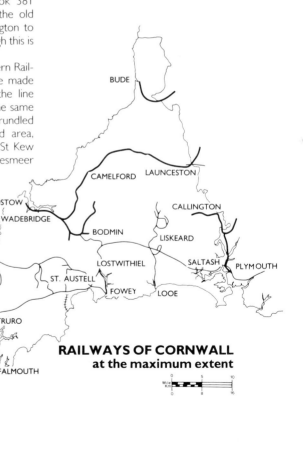

RAILWAYS OF CORNWALL
at the maximum extent

NATIONALISATION

FOLLOWING the first World War, when railways were under government control, there was a move for some rationalisation of the mass of small competing companies. This resulted in the grouping of all companies into just four, but since the one company which survived (although enlarged) was the GWR the effect of this in Cornwall was slight. From 1923 however, the L&SWR lost its identity, and for the next 25 years was to be part of the Southern Railway, whose territory stretched from Padstow to Dover, including all the south London suburban lines.

The problems which had been apparent when Cornwall's railways were planned in the 1840s were still with us in the 1940s. The county had little industry except china clay, and a population spread out in the rural areas, with few large towns—in 1948 there was no town with more than 20,000 people. There could never be an intensely used railway line within a county whose transport requirements were so diverse as to be better suited to the private car. But as with so many country branch lines, the introduction of railcars, reductions in station staff and economies in administration could have dramatically affected their viability.

Stagnation through the war and the early years of nationalisation, a total lack of any investment and the continuation of services much as they had developed in a pre-motorcar age, inevitably brought on the need for drastic action. A simple, if incredibly short-sighted decision, was made by British Rail and the government of the day. The acceptance of the 'Beeching Plan' brought the almost total closure of the former Southern Railway lines in Cornwall in 1966, and together with the end of some former GWR branches, at the same time, dramatically altered the railway map in a space of just a few years. Inadequate branch line services now limit the use of the main line itself and a goods service limited to the main Penzance route has affected the economic prospects of places such as Bude, over 40 miles from the nearest main line station. At the same time, over the past 40 years, those majority of passengers who use the mainline have seen a vast improvement in services and speeding up of times to London and the longer routes to the north. The *Cornish Riviera* reaches Exeter at an average of 90 mph and covers Paddington to Truro in 250 minutes (60 mph), compared with 333 minutes (45 mph) in 1961—although it no longer runs non-stop to Plymouth. Double glazing and air-conditioning make for pleasanter conditions, although open-plan carriages may not be preferred by all. The remaining branches continue with anything from 5 daily trains to Newquay up to 19 daily to St Ives, the diesel units providing a service little different from the last days of steam.

Attempts have been made to generate traffic elsewhere. A new station at Lelant Saltings provides a summer park-and-ride service for the motorist into congested St Ives. Otherwise much of the effort appears to be mere marketing ploys such as the introduction of the name 'Cornish Railways' with, for a short time, a Manager of Cornish Railways. But the actual organisation running railways in the west, since 1948, has seen so many changes that it would require a separate chapter to relate, as would the ever changing system of special fares and discounts for almost every class of traveller!

This scene at Penryn goods yard after the last war shows the busy traffic the railways once carried.

Cornish Studies Library

LOCOMOTIVES

The earliest railways were horse-drawn but the Bodmin & Wadebridge Railway became one of the earliest railways in Britain to adopt steam traction from the outset, in 1834. The first locomotive was named *Camel*, after the local river, and came from South Wales. Crude though it appears to us today, it was at the leading edge of the technology of the time.

Problems there were, of course, for such a pioneer in so remote a place. At one point its engineer stripped the locomotive down and rebuilt it to his liking to improve matters. Another problem was solved when it was found to have wheels of different sizes! Satisfaction was evidently attained and a second locomotive, named *Elephant* followed.

The Hayle Railway also used steam power from 1837 but rather less is known about these early locomotives. The first was said to have come from Liverpool and the second to have been built locally at Copperhouse Foundry, in Hayle. Both are said to have been capable of forty miles an hour. Three other locomotives followed before the railway became part of the West Cornwall Railway when they were joined by more up-to-date locomotives.

The Redruth & Chasewater and the Liskeard & Caradon railways bought their first locomotives in 1856 and 1862 respectively and these were ungainly machines from northern manufacturers. However they served their purposes well and all lasted well over fifty years.

Rather different locomotives appeared in the county on the opening of the Cornwall Railway to Truro in 1859. A contractor, and later the South Devon Railway, supplied the motive power for the new broad gauge line in the form of large 4-4-0 and 0-6-0 saddle tanks. Built in Bristol, they carried names such as *Elk*, *Hawk* and *Wolf* and were painted dark green. In due course the same engines worked the West Cornwall Railway and as the system extended so the number and types of engine, broad and standard gauges. Smaller 2-4-0 saddle tank engines were introduced for branch lines. Increasing traffic and the advent of GWR control brought some change but the GWR followed a very conservative policy on the broad gauge, particularly in view of its imminent demise. Some tank engines were converted to tender engines to take heavier trains and some new engines were built that could, in due course, be altered to standard gauge.

The Liskeard & Caradon's 1864 *Cheesewring* with a granite train at Moorswater, near Liskeard.

Castle class 5098 *Clifford Castle* near Chacewater with a local passenger train. 1961.

Following the change of gauge in 1892 standard GWR locomotives were used and the 'Duke' class of 4-4-0 designed especially for the west of England. These were followed by the 'Bulldog', 'Badminton' and 'Atbara' classes for passengers while the goods traffic was left to saddle tank engines.

When the L&SWR eventually reached into Cornwall in the 1890s they too employed 4-4-0 tender engines for passenger traffic and the elegant T9 'Greyhound' class survived until the 1960s. After the Great War the N class of 2-6-0, a sort of utility steam engine, took a major share on the North Cornwall line. At Wadebridge, however, due to the restrictions on the Wenford line, three charming little 2-4-0 well-tank engines survived, nicknamed after their designer, Beattie. Designed for fast suburban traffic out of Waterloo, they arrived at Wadebridge for 'retirement' in 1895 and stayed until 1962! Two have been preserved.

The steeply graded and sharply curved lines west of Exeter caused many operating difficulties for the railways and a number of locomotive classes were designed especially for the job. The Great Western 'Duke' class has been mentioned and the GWR followed it with the 'Hall' class of 4-6-0 in 1929. To a lesser extent the Southern Railway, successors to the L&SWR, followed suit. In the 1920s they were desperately short of engines for their western branch lines and rebuilt especially some engines into the EIR class of 0-6-2 tank. Later still Bulleid designed his outstandingly successful 'West Country' class of light Pacifics for the Southern lines to Ilfracombe, Bude and Padstow. The square stream-lining earned them the unkind and unjust nickname 'spam-cans'!

Traffic on the GWR lines was growing fast and larger and more powerful engines were designed to handle it, although the Royal Albert Bridge prevented the largest classes reaching

LSWR Adams 4-4-0 of 1884.

into Cornwall. Many of the classes introduced in the early years of this century lasted until the end of steam. On the branch lines the 45xx class of 2-6-2 tank became common from 1906, working to Helston, St Ives, Falmouth, Bodmin, Looe and Launceston. The ubiquitous and distinctive Great Western pannier tank looked after freight traffic on both main line and branches, as well as some passenger services.

On the main line services were taken over gradually by 2-6-0 mixed traffic engines but following their introduction in 1929 The 'Hall' class became the mainstay of the Cornish main line right through to the sixties, assisted by the later 'Grange' class and the powerful 'Castle' class. In 1945 the 'County' class was introduced and became popular once accepted. For heavy freight 2-8-0 locomotives made not infrequent visits to Cornwall and a couple of heavy 2-8-0 tanks were stationed at St Blazey to handle the clay traffic. British Railways standard classes, introduced after nationalisation, never made much impact in Cornwall apart from the 'Brittania' class 4-6-2 pacifics which often took the 'Cornish Riviera Express'.

The last steam train to Penzance, about to return to Plymouth. Untypically, the locomotive is an ex-Southern Railway 'Pacific' *Salisbury*. May 1964.

The first of the short-lived North British Warship class diesels D600 *Active* at St. Austell with a parcels train. 1962.

Traffic was never so heavy on what became the Southern Railway in Cornwall but was handled by the 'West Country' class, with help from the N class and later from one or two of the B.R. standard classes, such as class 4 mixed traffic 2-6-4 tank. On the branch lines to Bude, Callington and Bodmin North older L&SWR locos ruled the day, usually 0-4-4 tank engines of classes M7 or O2, until the 1950s when steam locomotives displaced from other parts of the country began to appear; in particular these were the L.M.S. design of 2-6-2 tank while, for a time, GWR pannier tanks took over the Bodmin branch.

In the late fifties steam began to be displaced by diesel power. Multiple unit railcars began to appear on the branch lines, although it must be admitted they gave superb views from their large windows. The Western Region of B.R. followed an individual, some say a Great Western, policy as regards dieselisation and introduced their own classes of diesel hydraulic locomotives. On the main line two classes of 'Warship' appeared, one built in Glasgow of which only five were built, and a more popular type based on a German design. Each was of 2,000 or 2,200 h.p. For the branch lines a half size version of the Glasgow design, of 1,000 or 1,100 h.p. was developed but these could also run in tandem on main line trains if need be.

The last steam train ran to Penzance in 1964, an enthusiasts' special hauled, ironically for a Great Western line, by a Southern stream-lined 'West Country' class engine. It was the end of 130 years of supremacy of steam on Cornwall's railways and crowds packed Penzance station to see the sight.

As the branch lines were whittled away and main line services reduced in variety and scope, so did the types of diesel locomotive. The diesel hydraulic types disappeared, after barely twenty years service, and standard diesel electric classes took their place. The Brush type 4, now know as Class 47, so common throughout the country took over many main line trains while Type 37s look after the freight and clay traffic. Virtually all long distance expresses, particularly to London, are operated by the High Speed Trains, the 125s, and other through trains by Class 50, the latter now bearing the names of the old 'Warships' so a diesel tradition has begun. On the remaining branch lines the old railcars still reign supreme. The new 'Sprinters' were tried but initially found lacking on Cornish grades and curves so, again, the individuality of Cornwall's railways made itself felt.

GAZETTEER

ONE WAY of viewing the features of the railways is to travel on the remaining lines, but this is not always the best way of seeing the viaducts and bridges which are often the most dramatic structures. However all the lines are worth travelling, particularly in one of the older diesel railcars which give a view of the track ahead—or behind, and there are some spectacular views of the countryside and coasts. It is surprising that British Rail have not promoted the branch lines more vigorously as tourist attractions in their own right, and one must speculate on the enormous potential for such lines as the St Ives branch for steam operation in the summer.

Cornwall's railways have seen drastic changes in the past twenty years; firstly from the effects of 'modernisation' and the Beeching Report and, secondly, from the ability of modern earth-moving machinery to sweep away in days what took years to achieve. As a result much of our railway heritage is to be found in the routes themselves, where the engineers' skills at putting their railways through an often difficult landscape can still be appreciated.

In recent years the renewal and modernisation of railway stations has resulted in the demolition of many original buildings dating back to the first opening of the lines. Unfortunately this process seems to be continuing, and although in some instances alterations have shown due respect for the better architectural features of the old, many good buildings are no longer in use and continue to be under threat. Some of the best early station buildings are those, especially in the east of the county on the main line, which have long been redundant and are simply boarded up. When demolition takes place, new sheds or shelters of no architectural merit are usually erected.

The earliest mineral lines, out of use for 70 years or so, often remain clearly visible in the countryside while other more recent lines are hard to trace, particularly where British Rail have sold off a strip of land to adjoining owners for incorporation into fields.

In many stations the only historic remains are in the letters 'GWR' which were incorporated into cast-iron work for platform seats, the brackets supporting platform canopies, bridges and other places. It is worth looking out for.the old monogram, which in many cases will date back to the end of the last century.

The Ordnance Survey maps indicate many of the old lines as the course of an old railway—or 'cse of old rly'. Grid references are given in this Gazetteer so you will find an Ordnance Survey Landranger map useful.

The ⇌ symbol indicates that the station or line is still open for passengers.

Remember, never trespass on the railway, for a moving train can be very dangerous if you are where you should not be. Even if the line is closed and the track gone it is almost certainly private property. Landowners are frequently helpful if your interest is genuine, but you should seek permission before entering their land.

Warship class diesel *Zebra* at Penzance with a summer express, 1961.

WHAT TO LOOK OUT FOR

The buildings that remain from the early days of Cornwall's railways are well worth looking out for as you travel the county, whether by rail, car or on foot. The earlier structures, station buildings, bridges, goods sheds and others, were built by local companies. They were very much in the local building tradition, making use of Cornish materials– essentially whatever was available in the locality– before the main railway line made it possible to import building materials economically. Slate roofs and stone walls are usual.

Often rough uncoursed stone was used, with cut blocks only for corners, dressing around doors and windows and for lintels, although an alternative was brick which, though not common, was available locally in most parts of the county. Given this simple range of materials, local builders produced straightforward functional buildings with little decoration, although the embellishments found in railway architecture 'up-country' would probably have been ruled out on cost grounds by most Cornish railway companies! The buildings and bridges which remain from before 1859 show little to distinguish them from harbour-side warehouses, farm buildings or road bridges of the period. With the coming of the Cornwall Railway and the L&SWR, changes did take place, for these railways could import materials easily, although local stone and slate did still predominate. Bridges could now be built of purple or deep red engineering bricks. Complete buildings could be built of imported red brick, such as Truro station, with its high-pitched roofs showing French gothic influences and a much more ornate style generally. It is only in these later buildings that any conscious 'architecture' is apparent, but it is the original buildings of the Cornwall Railway whose style is probably most to our modern taste. The surviving stations at Saltash, Menheniot and Penryn show simple and restrained stucco decoration in the Italianate style which was favoured by Brunel. As engineer to the Cornwall Railway, the design of these buildings would have been his responsibility and would have originated in his office. From the architectural point of view, one must regret that none of the modern replacement buildings appearar to be of any merit.

RAILWAY BRIDGES

Throughout the county there are smaller bridges worth looking out for, there are few of the elaborate Victorian structures found in some other areas. The railway companies did import building bricks to the county on a scale which would not have been possible for an organisation without its own transport, but local stone of various kinds was used extensively. Amongst the more interesting of the smaller bridges is that at Carlyon Bay [SW 055523]. A gothic castellated bridge, it takes the Cornwall Railway over the road to Carlyon Bay; built for the opening of the main line in 1859 it is still in use.

LEVEL CROSSINGS

Being short of capital and anticipating comparatively little traffic, many early lines in Cornwall were built with many level crossings before these were officially discouraged. Some of these are still in use today on the surviving branch lines, while others can still be traced with crossing keepers cottages alongside. On some better used lines, the road was later diverted and a bridge built either over or under the railway. Those in use today include one on the Newquay road, outside St Columb Road [SW 908596], crossing the former Cornwall Minerals Railway, with a picturesque keepers cottage; a number on the Liskeard and Looe line [SX 240634 and 249556]; and on the GWR main line, crossings at Camborne [SW 649397] and Gwinear Road [SW 613383]. Many examples can be traced on the disused lines, including that at Devoran, where the Redruth & Chacewater Railway crossing gates have been preserved and the keepers cottage has been used as a house for many years [SW 791394].

A freight train heads towards Wenford, in charge of one of the vintage Beattie tank locomotives.
Cornish Studies Library

The St. Blazey depot of the Cornwall Minerals Railway.

Outside Truro, on the Old Falmouth Road, at Calenick [SW 821432], the crossing gates remain and part of the original 1852 West Cornwall Railway route into Truro (Newham) forms a public footpath.

ST AUSTELL
[SX 016526]

Mainly unspoilt late Victorian station buildings; note the entwined 'GWR' monogram in cast-iron work on the footbridge.

ST BLAZEY
[SX 074537]

Here were the headquarters of the Cornwall Mineral Railway. A classic, planned, small railway company works, designed by one of the last great Victorian railway engineers, Sir Morton Peto, who was engineer of the railway, but was bankrupted through his financial involvement in its development.

The works was built for the opening of the line in 1874, and consists of a segment of a 'round-house' locomotive shed — with turn-table at the centre — of a size to take all the company's original 11 locomotives. This building is then connected by a small link to the long workshop block, with chimneys for blacksmiths forges etc.

Architecturally the complex is unusual for Cornwall, with its ornate red brickwork, but is a fine example of the period. It is still in use by BR and is a Listed Building. The loop connecting with Par station on the main line was built by the GWR in 1879.

BODMIN & WADEBRIDGE RAILWAY

One of Cornwall's early railways that were so full of character. Opened with steam power in 1834 from Wadebridge to Wenford Bridge (12 miles) with branches to Bodmin and Ruthern. Bought by the London & South Western Railway, in 1845, although not making a physical connection until its North Cornwall Railway reached Wadebridge in 1895. In the meantime the GWR had made a connection in 1888, via Bodmin General. The Bodmin to Wadebridge passenger service ceased in 1967 but clay traffic kept the Wenford line open until 1983, closure coming a year before the line's 150th anniversary.

The terminus in Bodmin has been swept away as have all the original buildings at Wadebridge, apart from some warehouses on the quay. At many of the original depots, where the company sold sea-sand as fertiliser, the wharfinger's house survives. Such places are Ruthern [SX 013668], Helland [SX 065715] and Tresarrett [SX 089732].

Picking its way between the houses at Helland, a 'Steam Farewell' special on the Wenford branch. 1964.

Bodmin North station in 1965. A railbus waits to leave.

BODMIN BRANCH (3½ miles)

Built to standard gauge by the GWR to connect the town to Bodmin Road station on the main line in 1887. Quite short and often disregarded, it is a very steep line and includes, at Bodmin Road, a sizable viaduct. The connection to Boscarne Junction and the Bodmin & Wadebridge Railway was made in 1888. Closed to passengers in 1967 and goods traffic in 1983 the line is now the subject of preservation proposals.

BODMIN GENERAL STATION
[SX 073663] A fine example of a country terminus, surviving almost intact, with its station buildings, signal box and engine shed, all dating from the 1880s. Well worth preserving.

BODMIN PARKWAY
[SX 110640]
Known as Bodmin Road until recent times this was the junction for the Bodmin branch. Station buildings destroyed, as has been the transshipment shed for transferring goods from broad gauge to narrow, and vice versa, but the private drive from Lanhydrock House (now National Trust) still sweeps up from the west of the station.

BROWN QUEEN TUNNEL
[SX 097570]
A short tunnel, 88 yards [73m], but noteworthy for being built for a double broad gauge track.

BUDE BRANCH (4½ miles in Cornwall)

Another line that just crosses the border into Cornwall. Bude was reached by the L&SWR from Holsworthy in 1898 and closed in 1966. The station site [SX 211059] has been cleared totally and redeveloped but the track of the harbour branch still makes a footpath to the canal basin.

BUGLE
[SX 017593]
A wooden shelter here adorns the platform. The Carbis branch, now a separate single line from Goonbarrow Junction, turns away after the station. This was the furthest point on Treffry's Par Railway, although he intended going further, and the route on to St Dennis Junction is CMR built. The CMR girder over-bridges on the line display the name of William West's St Blazey Foundry and are dated.

BURNGULLOW
[SW 982524]
The junction for one of the major clay branches although the station here closed many years ago. There is much to see, both defunct and active, of Cornwall's china clay industry that monopolises the landscape to the north. Many of the old coal-fired china clay dries still line the track at this point.

CALLINGTON BRANCH (8 miles in Cornwall)

The origin of this branch was the three and a half feet gauge East Cornwall Mineral Railway, opened in 1872 from Kelly Bray, north of Callington, to the quays at Calstock on the River Tamar. It carried freight and minerals only but in 1908 the route was incorporated in the standard gauge Plymouth, Devonport & South Western Junction Railway's branch to Callington, from their main line at Bere Alston, on the Devon side of the Tamar. The river was crossed by a new viaduct and the line then joined the route of the old ECMR. The incline

The overall roof at Callington station was quite distinctive. Here 41323 has arrived from Bere Alston in 1963.

down to Calstock quays was replaced by a steam hoist which carried standard gauge wagons down the side of the viaduct.

The line beyond Gunnislake closed in 1966 but passenger trains still run out from Plymouth as far as Gunnislake. Scenically, this is one of the most spectacular branch lines in the west country and well rewards a trip.

Callington station site [SX 360715] has been almost cleared but at Luckett [SX 385718] and Latchley [SX 407721] the original ECMR buildings survive, in use as private dwellings. Gunnislake station is now bare but there is more of interest at Calstock.

CALSTOCK
[SX 434688]

The village, clinging to the steep banks above the Tamar, is dominated by its viaduct [433686] completed for the opening of the line in 1908.

The viaduct was built of mass concrete block masonry which now appears almost indistinguishable from stone. The 11,000 blocks were made on site, on level land on the Devon bank, but problems arose when no solid foundation could be found for one of the river piers. Rock was eventually found at 120' [36m], and as a result the viaduct took 3½ years to build, considerably delaying the opening of the line. The 12 arches, each of 60' [18m] span, with a height of 117' [35·6m] has resulted in a good looking structure, even if it lacks the engineering significance of Brunel's bridge downstream at Saltash.

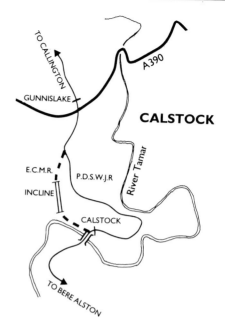

A Callington to Bere Alston train crosses into Devon at Calstock, 1963.

At the side of the viaduct, leading from the station, on the west side, can be seen the approach to the steam hoist which connected the line with the old ECMR sidings on the quay below, with the remains of steel girders set into the viaduct—although the hoist was removed in 1936. These sidings ran from the centre of the village along half-a-mile of quays, which chiefly exported stone and ore, to the bottom of the incline [SX 428689], now marked only by a bridge over the road, although the steep angle of the line can be seen here rising up the hillside. At the head of the incline [SX426695] the Incline Station buildings—the engine shed, water tower and incline house—remain an interesting group.

The incline head at Calstock showing the engine shed and water tower on left and incline house on right.

Camborne in 1967. A Western class diesel arrives with a London-bound train.

CAMBORNE STATION
[SW 649397]

The up station building survives, although now devoid of its canopies, and the goods shed, once an important part of any station, is now a building supplies depot. The level crossing here and at Roskear Junction, to the east, where the signal box is, have lifting barriers.

CAMBORNE & REDRUTH TRAMWAY (3½ miles)

Not strictly a railway but Cornwall's only electric street tramway and unique in Britain in running a mineral service. Opened in 1902 for passengers, the mineral trains started carrying tin ore through the streets for local mines in 1903. Whilst the passenger service gave way to competition from buses in 1927, the last mineral train did not run until 1934. The former office and waiting room can be seen at Redruth West End but the major survival is the former works and car sheds at Pool, now part of the Electricity Board works there [SW 664413]. In front of the National Trust's pumping engine at Taylor's Shaft, [SW 674418] also at Pool, are the remains of the ore bins that loaded the tramway wagons.

CHACEWATER STATION
[SW 741442]

Once the junction station for Perranporth and Newquay the down station building was replaced in the fifties following a fire. It is still there serving as an office for the cement company who use the goods yard. The two sidings are typical of what a country station would once have had.

CHACEWATER TO NEWQUAY

Built by the GWR and opened from Blackwater Junction [SW 733455], west of Chacewater station [SW 741442], to Perranporth (7¾ miles) in 1903; and extended to Shepherds (4½ miles) in 1905 where it connected with the mineral line from Newquay to give a through route to that resort. The line closed totally in 1963. St Agnes station [SW 722492], after lying derelict for some years, has been attractively restored as an industrial unit but the other stations have been demolished. Much of the route has been restored to agriculture but two viaducts remain at Goonbell [SW 732497] and near Perranwell [SW 773527]. Part of the trackbed near St Newlyn East is used by the Lappa Valley Railway.

THE CHINA CLAY LINES

Apart from the Treffry tramway which developed into the present day Newquay branch line, the considerable traffic in china clay resulted in a number of other branches which penetrated the heart of the 'clay country'. This is a fascinating part of Cornwall with a character of its own and unknown to many people, whether visitors or locals. Its surviving railways give a glimpse of what the mineral railways a century or more ago could have looked like and remains can be sought out with perseverance.

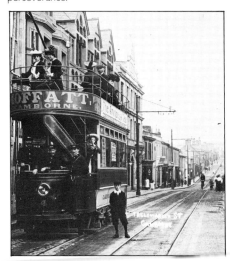

Camborne-Redruth Tramway Car No. 4 at Camborne.

CORNWALL'S RAILWAY HERITAGE

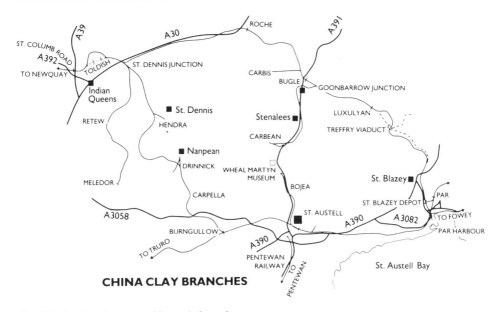

CHINA CLAY BRANCHES

The Meledor branch ran roughly south from St-Dennis Junction [SW 934599] and opened in 1876 as part of the Cornwall Minerals Railway. A GWR extension in 1912 added a further 1½ miles but it closed in 1983 and is lifted. To the east a line ran from St Dennis Junction through to Burngullow, but is now severed south of St Dennis. The lower section from Burngullow to Drinnick was opened as the broad gauge Newquay & Cornwall Junction Railway in 1869 while the upper part, that now lifted, was Treffry's northern line from Newquay Harbour, opened about 1850. There was an incline, still discernible, up to Hendra Downs [SW 951575].

From Bugle three branches left the CMR main Newquay line. Carbis Wharf [SX 002596] was the terminus of one and Wheal Rose [SX 015593] another. The first is still intact but unused while the second, little more than a siding, is long gone. The third line actually ran from Goonbarrow Junction [SX 023589] to Carbean [SX 003564] and was built by the Cornwall Minerals Railway opening in 1893. Most of it closed in 1965 but heavy clay traffic still originates close to the junction.

Running northwards from the Cornwall main line towards Carbean was the Trenance Valley line, one of the last GWR branches to be built, opened in 1920, although work on construction had begun before the Great War. This terminated at Bojea [SX 007550], a short distance from the Wheal Martyn China Clay Museum. It closed in 1964.

COPPERHOUSE BRIDGE
[SW 567383]

A tiny bridge over a narrow stream, on the Phillack side of Copperhouse Creek, built by the Hayle Railway. Notable for being built from slag blocks produced in the local copper smelting works, and also for being the earliest surviving railway bridge in the county, dating from 1837 although it has been disused since 1852.

CORNWALL RAILWAY (49¾ miles)

TRURO TO SALTASH

The Cornwall Railway took 13 years to raise the funds and build the main line Plymouth to Truro which was opened in 1859 as a broad gauge line. Even today the line carries many of the hallmarks of Brunel, in the stations and bridges and in the route itself.

Of the 34 viaducts which were called for to cross Cornish valleys, all but four are still in use. All of the viaducts were timber and were rebuilt between 1871 and 1908. Most were replaced with new masonry viaducts built alongside to avoid interruptions to traffic, and the old piers often remain. A few were replaced by embankments and there are also five tunnels, but the finest piece of engineering is, of course, the Royal Albert Bridge at Saltash.

Backed by the GWR, the Cornwall Railway was worked by the South Devon Railway and taken

The signal box at Perranwell, on the Falmouth branch, was quite unusual. The staion buildings and goods shed are of Cornwall Railway origin and behind the train can be seen a camping coach. 1962.

over by the GWR in 1889, being converted to standard gauge in 1892 along with all the broad gauge lines in the west of England.
It now forms part of the west of England main line and makes a fascinating journey today.

CORNWALL MINERALS RAILWAY

See Newquay Branch.

ST DENNIS JUNCTION
[SW 934599]

Now a shadow of its former self, the route of the two branches, to Retew and to Drinnick and Burngullow, can be seen on the south side of the line. From here on to Newquay the line is back on the route of Treffry's tramway.

DEVORAN

See Redruth & Chasewater Railway.

ST ERTH STATION ⇌
[SW 542358]

Originally named St Ives Road until the branch line to St Ives was opened in 1877, the station retains its buildings from that time and the branch is still open. The milk traffic to London, from the adjoining dairy here, was once very heavy.

FALMOUTH BRANCH (11¾ miles)

Originally intended as part of the main line of the broad gauge Cornwall Railway, the Truro to Falmouth section opened later, in 1863, and has always been operated as a branch. The more generous engineering of the broad gauge is often apparent. Eight of Brunel's timber viaducts survived until the 1920s and 1930s and the line now has four viaducts and two tunnels in its short length.

FALMOUTH: THE DELL ⇌
[SW 811321]

Opened in the 1960s and intended as the new terminus of the branch but resistance from the public and the train crews, who objected to stopping on the steep gradient, frustrated the official desire.

FALMOUTH STATION ⇌
[SW 818323]

The original overall roof here has long gone and only a length of canopy survives from the station building. From Castle Drive, behind the station, an excellent view can be had of the docks and fine natural harbour, the original goal of the railway's builders.

FOWEY
[SX 125522]

Fowey was approached by two separate railways. The first line into Fowey was the broad-gauge Lostwithiel & Fowey Railway, an impecunious company that could not raise the money to complete the job. They opened to Carne Point (4¾ miles) in 1869, intending to carry iron ore from Restormel Iron Mine, but did not get the traffic, and the railway fell out of use in 1879. The CMR took it over in 1893 and re-opened it as standard gauge in 1895. Never a great success, the line closed to passengers in 1965 but is now the only rail route to Fowey's deep water harbour and so survives for china clay traffic.

In the early years of this century the GWR invested heavily in new deep-water quays along the river just north of the town. The most up-to-date mechanised handling was available for tipping whole railway wagons of clay direct into ships' holds. The port of Fowey in recent years has been handling a million tons of clay a year, and even today a substantial part of this comes by rail.

The Cornwall Mineral Railway's line from St Blazey to Fowey, opened 1874, passed through Cornwall's longest tunnel, Pinnock [SX 105535], at 1,173 yards (1·07km) long. After closure in 1968 the route was converted into a private road to give clay lorries access to Fowey harbour, avoiding narrow roads and lanes which are particularly congested in the summer.

ST GERMANS
[SX 360575]

One of the original station buildings dating from 1859, showing the partiality Brunel had for the Italianate architectural style.

GOONBARROW JUNCTION
[SX 023589]

Now the intermediate point between St Blazey and Newquay, where the single line token is exchanged, and still busy with clay traffic despite the Goonbarrow branch being closed.

GUNNISLAKE
[SX 425712]

Nothing remains of the old station buildings, and so a cleared site, almost a mile from Gunnislake village, forms an unwelcoming end to the picturesque Tamar Valley line.

Gunnislake station in independent days.
Cornish Studies Library

HAYLE
[SW 560374]

The station building, engine shed and unusual tall signal box have all gone, but the route of the Hayle Wharves branch can be seen dropping steeply to cross the old main road. Beside this road is the swing bridge that carried the original Hayle Railway line over the entrance to Copperhouse creek, and back along to their original terminus which was under the present day Hayle viaduct. On this last line horses were still used for shunting wagons in the early 1960s.

THE HAYLE RAILWAY (26¾ miles)

Standard gauge mineral railway running from the port of Hayle to Portreath, Redruth, dating from 1837. The level sections were worked by locomotives but were connected by rope-hauled inclines at Angarrack, Penponds, Portreath and on the Tresavean branch. The last has been filled in but that at Angarrack can be seen from the road to the village of the same name, just off the A30 to the east of Hayle.

Parts of the former routes can be followed, particularly in Hayle along the north side of Copperhouse creek (see Copperhouse), but the West Cornwall Railway rebuilt much between Hayle and Redruth and little else remains.

A train for Helston leaves Gwinear Road in June 1962, in charge of 'Prairie' tank 5562.

Diesel locos had replaced steam in this 1962 study of the Cober Viaduct on the Helston branch.

HELSTON BRANCH (8¾ miles)

A local company, the Helston Railway, opened in 1887 to standard gauge, but the GWR worked the line from the outset and took over in due course. The first GWR motor services ran from Helston to the Lizard in 1903, one of the first examples in the country of a rural bus service. All the intermediate stations have been demolished and parts of the route filled in. The names of these stations were particularly delightful: Praze-an-Beeble, Nancegollan and Truthall Halt. The Cober Viaduct [SW 664297] still stands. Closed to passengers in 1962 and goods the following year.

ST IVES BRANCH (4¼ miles)

Opened by the GWR in 1877 this was the last broad-gauge line to be built. The views across St Ives Bay alone make a trip worthwhile. St Ives and Carbis Bay stations have been demolished but Lelant [SW 548373] survives as a private residence, convenient for the trains!

It is hard to see how the wooden shed and breeze block and corrugated iron shelter at Carbis Bay give a better 'modern image' than the stone buildings they replaced. Part of the line runs through a rock cutting so hard that miners had to be employed to get the line through. Goods services were withdrawn in 1963.

Some of the best views in Cornwall can be had from a train, as the passengers on this train found as they approached St. Ives in summer 1961.

LARGIN & WEST LARGIN VIADUCTS

To save the cost of rebuilding these viaducts yet again, the track has been singled to save weight on the structure.

A train with 4555 waits at Launceston station to return to Plymouth, 1962. This is the ex-L.S.W.R. station which was latterly shared with G.W.R. trains.

LAUNCESTON BRANCH (1¾ miles in Cornwall)

The Launceston & South Devon Railway extended the broad gauge Plymouth to Tavistock branch to Launceston in 1865. Just reaching into Cornwall, the terminus was the only station in the county. Trains were switched to the adjacent L&SWR station in 1952 until closure in 1962.

The site [SX 331850] has been cleared totally and is now the car park of the Launceston Steam Railway, a narrow gauge line of quite a different character.

LISKEARD
[SX 248637]

An unusual layout, with the lines running through a deep cutting with station buildings at a much higher level, while close to the east end of the up platform, virtually at right-angles, is the Looe branch platform.

LISKEARD VIADUCT
[SX 250 635]

At 150' [45·7m], this is the second highest of the original timber viaducts on the Cornwall Railway, 240 yds [219m] long and replaced by the present masonry structure in 1896. The loop line of 1901 connecting the main line at Liskeard Station with the Liskeard and Looe passes below, forming the present-day Looe branch. The viaduct can be seen from Liskeard By-Pass.

LISKEARD & CARADON RAILWAY

Built to enable the copper mines and granite quarries of the Caradon Hill area to get the produce to Moorswater and the Liskeard & Looe Canal, the railway opened fully in 1846. Its sinuous course was designed to maintain the grade so that trains could run down the line by gravity. Steam locomotives were introduced in 1862. Closure of the mines in 1885 was a major blow but it struggled on until taken over by the GWR in 1909. They closed it in 1917.

The lower part of the route has been overgrown for many years and parts absorbed into fields but the upper section is ideal for walking and exploration, with many fine stretches of granite sleeper blocks. Some of the bridges survive and these can be picked out on the Ordnance Survey map. An excellent walk is the circuit around Caradon Hill, starting at Minions [SX 261712] or Crow's Nest [SX 264694], and this takes in the Gonamena incline [SX 262704] and Tokenbury Corner depot [SX 280699].

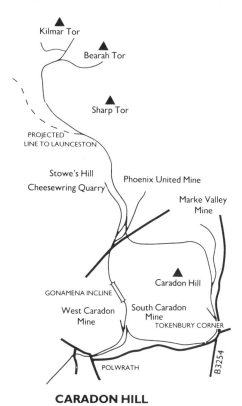

CARADON HILL

In 1907 the Liskeard & Caradon's Phoenix branch came to life again when the mine was reworked.

The branches to East Caradon and Marke Valley mines can be seen north of the latter point.
From Minions the line north to Cheesewring Quarry [SX 259723] can be followed, although the railway remains in the quarry have been destroyed in recent years. Also from Minions, and below the quarry dumps, runs the Kilmar Tramway, past Sharptor, and out onto the moor to Kilmar Tor [SX 252747] and Bearah Tor [SX 259745], a pleasant afternoon's walk. Running north-west from Sharptor the proposed route of an abortive extension of 1884 to Launceston is clearly visible as far as Rushyford Gate.

LONDON & SOUTH WESTERN RAILWAY

See North Cornwall Railway, Bude Branch, Callington Branch.

LOOE BRANCH ⇌

The Liskeard & Looe Union Canal Company opened the route from Moorswater to Looe in 1827 and replaced it with a railway in 1860, acting as an extension of the Liskeard & Caradon Railway. Passenger traffic was introduced in 1879. In 1901 the loop connection to the main line at Liskeard was opened, giving a new boost to the line and to Looe. The GWR ran the line from 1909, taking over the company in 1923. Freight traffic was withdrawn in 1963, apart from clay traffic from Moorswater, but the passenger service continues.
At Liskeard [SX 248637] one has the almost unique experience of departing from the branch platform facing north, turning through nearly 360° and then reversing direction at Coombe Junction [SX 239635] to continue one's journey southwards! The line continues north of Coombe for half a mile to Moorswater [SX 235643] where it once connected

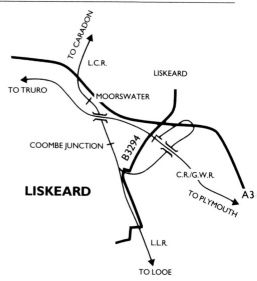

LISKEARD

with the Liskeard & Caradon Railway and where the works were. Now just the siding into the china clay dry survives, all the rest having been cleared for the by-pass and the industrial estate.
After leaving Coombe southwards the train runs alongside the remains of the canal, and the winding nature of the journey reveals the mineral railway origins. The bridges were rebuilt by the GWR in 1910 but the triple arches accommodating rail, river and canal can be seen. At Looe the station has been moved away from the town and replaced by a 'bus-shelter'. It is now hard to believe that trains once ran down the east quays almost to the Banjo Pier and that those quays were once stacked high with copper ores, coal and granite. On the seaward side of East Looe, high above the town, earthworks can be found of the start made by the GWR, in 1935, for a new direct branch from St Germans.

Train and station staff pose at Looe on Great Western engine No. 13, about 1910.

LOSTWITHIEL
[SX 106597]

Although both station buildings here have been demolished the impressive buildings which can be seen on the north are part of the former Cornwall Railway works. A wooden station building, a Listed Building, was here until removed by a so-called enthusiast and subsequently destroyed. This is the junction for the Fowey branch, still heavily used by long china clay trains.

MARAZION
[SW 507313]

Now closed but the down side station building survives as do a number of former Pullman carriages, relics of the days when you could spend your holiday in a 'Camping Coach' at a seaside or country station.

MENHENIOT
[SX 289613]

Another of Brunel's Italianate designs and, like St Germans, a pleasant survival of a typical modest country station.

MOORSWATER VIADUCT
[SX 237640]

A very elegant looking viaduct which is seen from the west end of the Liskeard By-Pass; rebuilt in 1881, and spanning the former Liskeard & Looe Railway, which now survives as a goods branch to Moorswater china clay dries. The viaduct is 318 yards (291 metres) long and 147' [44·8m] long.

NEWQUAY BRANCH

This line's origins go back to the 1830s when parts of it were built by J.T.Treffry, but the line as it is today was constructed by the Cornwall Minerals Railway. The CMR was part of a grand scheme to extract iron-ore from the Great Perran Iron Lode, between Perranporth and Newquay, and export it from Fowey. Treffry's Tramways were bought and reconstructed, and a connecting line built between. Extensions were made to Treamble for the iron mines and to Fowey harbour. In addition branches were built to Retew and Carbis and the whole system of 43½ miles opened in 1874.
Alas, the iron ore traffic did not materialise and the growing china clay industry was not enough to save the company so it handed over its working to the GWR in 1877, although the company retained its independence until 1896. A passenger service had been started in 1876. The GWR developed both the clay traffic and also the tourist business, putting a lot of effort into boosting Newquay as a holiday resort. The line is still open and a trip over it soon reveals its origins as a mineral railway.

NEWQUAY STATION
[SW 816618]

Now just a single line runs into Newquay station, once the terminus for through expresses; the length of the platform gives a clue to the former traffic here. The original CMR building still stands on the east side of the station.
Towards the end of the last century Newquay came to prominence as a holiday resort, large hotels being built to exploit the magnificent cliff scenery and the established railway connection. Through trains from Paddington began in the 1890s and by the 1950s several crowded double-headed trains—up to 15 carriages long—were arriving in the resort on summer Saturdays

NEWQUAY HARBOUR LINE
[SW 806620 to 816618]

Many years before the holiday makers arrived, this was the northern terminus of Treffry's tramway. To export minerals, particularly china clay from around St Dennis, it was necessary to take these loads direct down to the harbour; so the railway continued across Cliff Road along the footpath behind the Victoria Hotel and then along the present Manor Road before descending, as a cable-worked incline, in a tunnel to the harbour, where the lines divided to serve the quays. One line went out on a timber viaduct to the jetty, built in 1872, which still exists as an 'island' in the middle of the harbour. At its peak in the 1870s, Newquay ship-owners had 160 merchant vessels, but trade decreased towards the end of the century, and the last loads went to the harbour by rail in 1926.

Newquay station, the single railcar having arrived from Par.

NEWQUAY: TRENANCE VIADUCT
[SW 818612]

Originally built for the Treffry tramway as a timber structure similar to Brunel's 'fan viaducts' on the Cornwall Railway, it was rebuilt with wrought-iron girders by the Cornwall Minerals Railway in 1874 and then again, with heavy holiday traffic in mind, in its present masonry form in 1939.

NORTH CORNWALL RAILWAY

The L&SWR's ambitions to reach Cornwall from its Waterloo terminus took many years to achieve. Its protégé, the North Cornwall Railway, opened the line in sections; from Halwill Junction to Launceston in 1886, to Tresmeer in 1892 and Delabole in 1893. Wadebridge was reached in 1895 and Padstow finally in 1899. Closure was swifter; Halwill to Wadebridge in 1966 and Wadebridge to Padstow, as part of the Bodmin closures, a few months later in 1967.

Of all Cornwall's railways this line has more original buildings surviving than any other, probably because the L&SWR included living accommodation in many of their station buildings. Wadebridge [SW 991722], a joint L&SWR/GWR building, is an exception, which is now being converted into the John Betjeman Centre. St Kew Highway [SX 751031] is now an attractive guest house and most other stations are making very desirable private houses. The buildings are all to the same basic design but of different materials; some of brick, others of stone while a few are slate-hung. Not just the station buildings survive, but also waiting shelters, goods sheds and sometimes station signs. Tresmeer [SX 222886] is a fine example.

There were few engineering works of any significance on the North Cornwall route, despite rising up from Launceston, along the Kensey valley, to reach over 850' above sea level before descending to Wadebridge.

The signalman hands out the token to a train leaving Wadebridge for Bodmin Road. 1961.

Camelford station, on the former North Cornwall line.

Launceston station [SX 331850], like the GWR station alongside, is now demolished; the trackbed towards Egloskerry is now used by the delightful two-foot gauge Launceston Steam Railway, so one can still travel by steam over part of the North Cornwall line, albeit it in a very different manner than of old.

A mixed passenger and freight train runs alongside the River Camel and crosses Petherick Creek on its way to Padstow. 1964.

PADSTOW
[SW 921751]

The final extent of the L&SWR, reached in 1899, and furthest terminus of the *Atlantic Coast Express*, 260 miles from Waterloo. Here the L&SWR built the Metropole Hotel, trying to encourage holiday traffic, as the GWR was successfully doing at Newquay.

The line from Wadebridge ran along the Camel estuary, but crossed one creek with an impressive bridge at SW 925741.

PAR ⇌
[SX 077541]

Junction for the Newquay branch and in very original condition with stone buildings on the down side and full canopies on both platforms. At the time of writing the signal box and semaphore (mechanical) signals are all still in use.

PENRYN ⇌
[SW 779347]

The original station building in the Italianate design favoured by Brunel survives but in a sorry state. Covered in graffiti and boarded up one suspects it is looking for an excuse to be demolished. Due to a re-alignment of the tracks it is set back some distance.

Former Cornwall Railway station building at Penryn.

THE PENTEWAN RAILWAY

Cornwall's only true narrow gauge railway was opened in 1829 as a privately built line to serve Pentewan harbour, constructed by the Hawkins estate. Horse drawn, it was probably of about 4 feet 6 inches gauge initially but was rebuilt to 2 feet 6 inches in 1874 when locomotives were introduced. Closure came in 1918.

The St Austell terminus [SX 010523] has been built on but now carries a plaque recording the railway's existence. South of the A3058 the course can be clearly seen alongside the B3273 road to Mevagissey as far as Iron Bridge [SX 012512]. Here the route crossed to the east side of the road and followed the river to Pentewan harbour [SX 012472]. There are many interesting remains but those of railway interest actually date from the later internal railway of the concrete block sand company that operated here.

PENZANCE ⇌
[SW 476307]

The most westerly station in Britain, 326 miles from Paddington by the original route through Bristol. It still retains the overall roof that befits its position as Cornwall's counterpart to Paddington, although it has been rebuilt a few times since opening. The station interior is spoilt by some modern accretions that now occupy the former concourse area. Most of the clutter of surrounding buildings of Victorian times has gone; the engine shed was moved east to Long Rock but that too has now been demolished. The Travelling Post Office train that runs each weekday night can usually be seen in the carriage sidings during the day; it has now reverted to its Post Office red livery.

ST PINNOCK VIADUCT
[SX 178 647]

The highest of the Cornwall Railway's Brunel timber viaducts, at 151' [46m]–and 211 yds [193m] long. The original structure was replaced by one built entirely in masonry in 1880. The viaduct stands on the lane from Trago Mills out-of-town shopping centre to Middle Taphouse.

PORTREATH TRAMROAD

An early plateway whose first sod was cut in 1809 and which fell out of use after 1855. The Crofthandy terminus [SW 738425] has its cottage but other remains have been interfered with. A good deal of the route can be walked, with sleeper blocks often visible, and at Forge [SW 697457] an embankment, now carrying a road, is the line's major feature. At Portreath harbour [SW 656454] later developments have obliterated all trace. One remarkable survival is the Directors' carriage, now owned by the Trevithick Society and on display at Geevor Mining Museum. This is probably the oldest railway passenger vehicle in the world.

PORTREATH INCLINE

The incline built in 1837 by the Hayle Railway is clearly visible leading up the west side of the valley; its engine house [SW 658447] is now converted to a dwelling. The line, leading down to extensive sidings in the harbour area—now 'infilled' with housing—was in use until 1936.

QUINTRELL DOWNS ⇌
[SW 848604]

A rare survival of a corrugated iron waiting shed, once common throughout the GWR system. This section of the branch, with its many level crossings and tight boundaries, betrays more than anywhere the line's origins in an early mineral tramway. Slate slab fencing can be seen in places and elsewhere the railway is supported on stone walling. Although the level crossings have been modernised many of the gatekeeper's houses are still extant.

REDRUTH ⇌
[SW 701420]

Both station buildings survive with their canopies so the station retains much of its old character. Below the station is a corrugated iron, former GWR, bus garage.
The original Hayle Railway terminus later became Redruth Goods Yard, but has now been converted into a local authority car park, opposite the entrance to the Penventon Hotel [SW 694419].

REDRUTH & CHASEWATER RAILWAY (9½ miles)

Cornwall's first true railway, built to connect the mines of Gwennap with the sea at Devoran. Of four feet gauge and initially horse drawn it opened from Wheal Buller, near Redruth, to Devoran in 1826 and extended into Redruth and to Point in 1827. Closure came in 1915.

Stone sleeper blocks at the end of the Redruth & Chasewater Railway in Redruth.

At Devoran [SW 794390], the company's workshops are now the village hall and behind them the offices can be seen. Many of the quays from which copper was shipped are now built over, but the pattern can be visualised. Where the line crossed the present A39 road a level crossing gate is preserved, although the gate keeper's house has been demolished. At Twelveheads [SW 761419] a sizable embankment crosses the valley and a larger one at Hale Mills [SW 751424] was for a branch to Wheal Busy which was never completed. At Carharrack the line threads through the village, past Railway Terrace, and a small footbridge [SW 730412] has been recently restored. The Redruth terminus [SW 703421] can be seen. Many sections of the line can be walked or driven over and the stone blocks that carried the rails can be found in many places.

The former offices at Devoran of the Redruth & Chasewater Railway.

SALTASH: ROYAL ALBERT BRIDGE
[SX 435587]

One of Brunel's masterpieces. Construction lasted a little over eight years and much of the more complex work was supervised personally by Brunel. Each of the two spans is 455 feet (139 metres) and the overall length is some 730 yards (667 metres). There are seventeen side spans, leading to the two main spans, and the rails are 190 feet (58 metres) above the foundation of the central pier, the highest point of the structure being 260 feet (79 metres). The bridge was strengthened in 1903, 1930 and 1960.

The station still retains its original 1859 building on the up platform; these have now passed to another owner, and, hopefully, with a new use their future is more assured.

TOLDISH TUNNEL
[SW 920600]

Between St Dennis Junction and St Columb Road [SW 911596] the Treffry line passed through Toldish Tunnel. To save enlarging the tunnel the CMR diverted around to the north and both approaches to the tunnel can be seen from the train.

TREFFRY'S TRAMWAYS

Joseph Treffry was an astute businessman who came into large estates in mid-Cornwall and developed them in a very enterprising way. He bought Newquay harbour and built Par harbour and set about connecting his estates to these harbours. At Par he built a canal to Ponts Mill [SX 073563] connecting with a standard gauge railway which ascended the 1 in 10 Carmears incline. Power for the incline was by a waterwheel, fed by a leat that crossed the valley with the railway on the Treffry Viaduct [SX 056572], an unusual combined aqueduct and viaduct of ten arches. A branch of the railway to Colcerrow quarry provided the granite for the viaduct, which was completed in 1842, and other branches came into use before 1840. The railway, which was horse-drawn, ran on beyond the viaduct to Bugle. From Luxulyan the CMR took over the route.

At Newquay Treffry's tramway was opened in 1849, with one branch going to Wheal Rose lead mine and the other to Hendra Down, near St-Dennis, in the clay district. Most of these routes were taken over by the CMR and so are still in use today. The remains of the former incline at Hendra [SW 951572] may be found with diligent searching.

TREFFRY VIADUCT & LUXULYAN VALLEY
[SX 056572]

The CMR-built line takes a tortuous route through the valley to avoid the Carmears incline and passes beneath the Treffry viaduct. Of the earlier Treffry works, little can be seen of the canal at Ponts Mill [SX 073563] but the incline can be readily found running up the east side of the valley. The various branches both above the incline and on the floor of the valley make extremely pleasant walking in a beautiful wooded setting. The magnificent viaduct

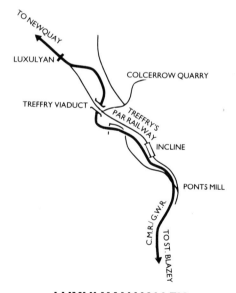

LUXULYAN VALLEY

itself is preserved and can be crossed on foot. At the head of the incline the wheelpit is clearly visible and remains of machinery abound, from a china stone mill that later used the site.

Truro station, G.W.R.

City of Truro at Truro. The record-breaking Great Western locomotive on show with an exhibition train on the inauguration of commercial television. 1961.

TRURO
[SW 818449]

Truro's station buildings date from the 1890s and have been renovated in recent years. The engine sheds and wagon works to the west of the station have been demolished, but the passenger service ensures that the atmosphere of a busy station remains. Truro Viaduct is the second viaduct east of the station—the first is Carvedras—and is the longest in Cornwall at 443 yards (405 metres). Both Truro and Carvedras Viaducts were rebuilt in 1904. Three miles west of Truro station is Polperro Tunnel, the longest on the main line, although not the longest in Cornwall, at 581 yards (531 metres).

The name of Truro will be remembered in the annals of locomotive history, for the GWR's *City of Truro* was the first locomotive in the country to travel in excess of 100mph. She achieved 102 mph in 1904 and has been preserved.

TRURO NEWHAM
[SW 830440]

The original terminus in Truro became a branch line from Penwethers Junction after the West Cornwall Railway diverted most of its trains into the new Cornwall Railway station at Truro in 1859. Passenger traffic ceased in 1863 but goods traffic not until 1971. Only one riverside warehouse now remains and the site is ripe for redevelopment.

The engine shed and wagon works, now demolished, at Truro provide the backdrop for ex-Great Western pannier tank 3709 and its local goods train. 1961.

THE WEARDE DEVIATION

Between St Germans and Saltash most of the original line ran somewhat to the south, close to the St Germans River. This section included five timber viaducts, all fairly low and entirely of timber due to the deep mud in the creeks they crossed. When the line was doubled in 1908 it was decided to cut out this section and a new line was built to the north, with three new masonry viaducts and a tunnel, Shillingham Tunnel [SX 392575], 452 yards (413 metres) long. The old line was then abandoned and its timber viaducts dismantled.

WEST CORNWALL RAILWAY (28½ miles)

TRURO TO PENZANCE

Opened by the West Cornwall Railway in 1852 utilising part of the Hayle Railway route (see below) and extended from Highertown at Truro to Newham in 1855. It was taken over by the Great Western Railway in 1866 when a third rail was added to permit broad-gauge trains to run through. It became part of the GWR main-line from Paddington to Penzance and as such is still open.

Wacker engine shed.

MISCELLANEOUS OTHER RAILWAYS

Very many of the mines, quarries and china clay workings that abound in Cornwall had their own railways, as did several of the harbours and quite a few other industries. Some had a steam engine or two, rather more possessed small diesel locomotives and even more made do with hand propelled wagons. Such railways are beyond the scope of this book but a few sites are worth mentioning.
At Wheal Martyn China Clay Museum [SX 004555], near St Austell, there is preserved a small steam locomotive, Judy, which for more than thirty years was at Par Harbour. Poldark Mine [SW 683316], near Helston, has a steam locomotive from Falmouth Docks. In the east of Cornwall, close beside the A374 Torpoint road, at Wacker Quay [SX 389551], is an engine shed and a description of the former railway that once served the military forts at Tregantle.

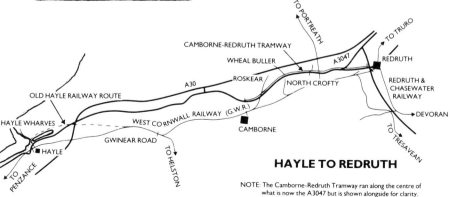

HAYLE TO REDRUTH

NOTE: The Camborne-Redruth Tramway ran along the centre of what is now the A3047 but is shown alongside for clarity.

Par station, with a Newquay train on the left.

FURTHER READING

Anthony, G.H.   *The Hayle, West Cornwall & Helston Railways*   Oakwood Press 1968
           The Tavistock, Launceston & Princetown Railways   Oakwood Press 1971
Barham, L.F.   *Cornwall's Electric Tramcars*   Glasney Press 1972
Barton, D.B.   *The Redruth & Chasewater Railway*   Bradford Barton 1966
Booker, F.   *Industrial Archaeology of the Tamar Valley*   David & Charles 1971
Clinker, C.R.   *The Railways of Cornwall 1809-1963*   David & Charles 1963
Drew, J.H.   *Rail & Sail to Pentewan*   Twelveheads Press 1986
Fairclough & Shepherd   *Mineral Railways of the West Country*   Bradford Barton 1975
Fairclough & Wills   *Southern Branch Line Special No.1 Bodmin & Wadebridge 1834-1978*
           Bradford Barton 1979
Lewis, M.J.T.   *The Pentewan Railway*   Twelveheads Press 1981
MacDermot, E.T.   *History of the Great Western Railway*   Ian Allan 1964
Messenger, M.J.   *Caradon & Looe; the Canal, Railways and Mines*   Twelveheads Press 1978
Reade, L.   *The Branch Lines of Cornwall*   Atlantic 1984
Thomas, D.St.J.   *West Country Railway History*   David & Charles
           The Country Railway   Penguin 1979
Woodfin, R.J.   *The Centenary of the Cornwall Railway*   Ely 1960

Front cover: Western Class Diesel on Penwethers Viaduct.   *John Wells*

ISBN 0 906294 16 9   © John P Stengelhofen 1988
All rights reserved. No part of this publication may be reproduced or transmitted in any form or by any means without the prior written permission of the publisher.
First published 1988 by Twelveheads Press, Chy Mengleth, Twelveheads, Truro, Cornwall TR4 8SN